Illustrations by Audeva Joseph and Millie Walton
Published by Simone Morris Enterprises, Norwalk, CT
ISBN: 979-8-9898972-4-7
Printed in the United States of America

REMEMBER ME, GRAMMY P.

A Story of How a Grandparent's Dementia is a Child's Journey Too!

Written By
Simone E. Morris
& Millie Walton

Illustrated By
Audeva Joseph
& Millie Walton

PATRICIA D. EDWARDS

MARCH 1, 1938 - FEBRUARY 11, 2024

This book is dedicated to
the beloved matriarch of our family,
Patricia D. Edwards, aka Grammy P.

We love and miss you dearly
and will continue to honor your legacy.

Acknowledgments

To My Daughter, Millie,
We are on a learning journey together.
We love each other fiercely.
Your kindness, empathy and talent inspire me daily.
I encourage you to stay curious and courageous.

To My Love, Stephen,
Thank you for your support on this journey.
You always demonstrate love and support for our family.
Your thoughtful input to the creation
and editing of this book was invaluable.
We appreciate you!

To My Loving Family,
Dementia has impacted us all.
It's a journey we'll never forget.
I love you all. #familyforever

Hi Reader,

I hope you enjoy this book because it is about how I learned about my grandma's dementia. It was hard for me, but I learned about it, and I hope you will, too, to see how other people are affected by it. I made drawings because I thought they could be in the story, and I thought I wanted to be an artist, too.

~Millie

Dear Parent, Caregiver, and Educator,

Thank you for purchasing our book. Writing a children's book about dementia felt like the right thing to do. The project was a labor of love, allowing space for us to navigate and process the dementia journey impacting the beloved matriarch of our family. To take the pain and turn it into purpose was cathartic for our family. We are proud to share our story and sincerely hope it will help anyone going through a similar journey.

My best advice is to be kind to yourself and your family on the journey. Love on one another. If you enjoyed the story, share it with others. We also hope you'll leave us a review wherever you can. We will continue to update the remembermegrammyp.com site with dementia resources we discover and find helpful.

~Simone

"Hi Millie!"
"Hi Mom!"
"How was school today?" Mom asked.
"Great," replied Millie.
"What was great about it," asked Mom.
"I loved art class," replied Millie.
Mom replied, "Did you draw anything special today?"
"I drew an anime cat. Mom, are there any snacks?"

Mom passed Millie's snack bag back to her.
"Thanks, Mom," replied Millie.
As Millie opened the snack bag, she asked, "What are we going to do now? And do you have my tablet?"
"Yes, it's in your snack bag. Grammy P. is coming over today," replied Mom.

"Great! Can we go to the playground for just a little while first?" requested Millie.

"Yes, Sweetie, we can, but we can't stay long because we need to meet Grammy P. and her aide Juana at our home. Daddy is there to meet Juana for drop off until we come home, but I promised I'd be back in time to make dinner. We can stay at the playground for forty-five minutes."

Millie got out of the car and ran toward the jungle gym. Millie made a new friend who also likes the jungle gym. Time moved swiftly and Mom called out to Millie, "It's time to get going, Sweetie!"

“Ahhhhh Mom, do we have to go? Ten more minutes, please?” requested Millie.

“OK,” offered Mom but she gave Millie a silent look that said don’t ask again for more time.

The next time Mom called, Millie was ready to go.

Millie and Mom left the park and headed home. Upon arrival at home, Mom unlocked the door. The family exchanged greetings.
Millie was the first to say, "We're home!"
"Hi, Millie." "Hi Sweetheart!" said Dad.
"Hi Honey, Hi Mom!" echoed Mom to Millie's Dad, and Grammy P.
Millie ran forward to express her greetings. She first hugged her dad and then turned to Grammy P.

"Oh, good, Grammy P., you're here!" Millie joyously uttered as she hugged her grandmother.
Mom headed to the kitchen, appreciative of her oh-so-happy family that always showed their affection.
Mom moved forward with dinner preparations.

Millie hung back with Grammy P. and Dad to give a school update and steer Dad and Grammy P. to watch her favorite show, *Family Reunion* on TV.

After *Family Reunion,* Millie switched over to watch an episode of *Just Add Magic.* If she's lucky, she might also squeeze in an episode of *K.C. Undercover* before dinner.

Grammy P. was all smiles, didn't fuss, and instead dozed off on the couch. Dad, meanwhile, spent time snuggling with Millie watching her shows.

Dad came in to set the table and talk with Mom while she finished preparing dinner. He took a seat at the dinner table.

"Please call Millie and Grammy P. to come in for dinner," asked Mom. Dad got up to gather each for dinner.

When they both entered the kitchen, Dad ushered Grammy P. to get settled in the chair by the window.

Mom asked Millie to get utensils and water for everyone at the table. Millie smirked. She and mom exchanged looks.

Millie then replied cheerfully, "Okay Mom," and took care of the tasks Mom asked her to do.

Everyone sat at the dinner table and held hands to complete a full circle.

"Can I pray tonight?" asked Millie.

"Certainly!" replied Mom.

"God is good, God is great, Let us thank him for our food. Amen."

Meanwhile, Dad interjected and added closing remarks to Millie's prayer. "Health, Wealth, and a clean green earth."

Everyone added in unison "Amen."

The family opened their eyes and proceeded to eat their meal.

"Can I go get our favorite game?" requested Millie. Mom said yes and Millie hurried to get the Trouble® game and returned to the dinner table.

When Millie returned, she took her seat. While eating, she removed the game from the box.
Millie said I call Red! Mom called Green and Dad selected Blue. Grammy P. got the last color, Yellow.

Grammy P. smiled and used her fork to pick up little bites of her food.
Dad and Mom continued eating and talking.

Meanwhile, Millie was wondering why Grammy was eating so slowly. Grammy P. loved family time. She could take games or leave them. She didn't see the big deal of playing a game over dinner. But still, she typically participated in the meal with more enthusiasm.

TROUBLE

After what seemed like forever to Millie, Dad got out the paper that outlined the game rules. "I'll review these for all of us," said Dad.

Millie already knew the rules and was anxious to get started.
Millie said, "I want to go first!"

But Mom insisted they all roll the dice to see who went first.

All three rolled, but when it came to Grammy P.'s turn, she seemed to have forgotten how to roll a die. With a little coaxing and instructions from Dad, she popped the Trouble® circle that rolled her turn at the die.

Grammy P. looked baffled when it was her turn to play the game.

"Your turn Grammy P.!" encouraged Millie gently.

Grammy P. didn't make any movement to roll the die or move her yellow piece on the game board.

Dad explained the game again and helped Grammy P. move one of her game pieces.

The game continued with pauses each time Grammy P.'s turn came around.

It seemed that when Grammy P.'s turn came, Grammy P. had forgotten the rules.

Mom explained the rules and what Grammy P. should do next. Grammy P. picked up her game piece and held it in her hand.

Mom gave more instructions on how to play the game and Grammy P. complied to do what Mom said to do.

When Grammy P.'s turn came again, she seemed confused all over again by the game.

Millie said with frustration, "Grammy P., we just told you the rules."

The game was no longer fun for Millie. She said, "Can we finish the game now?"

"Ok Sweetie, pack it up and put it back where you got it from. And then we'll get ready for bed."

As Millie put the game away, she was disappointed the family didn't seem to have the usual fun playing Trouble®. She was also a little confused about what was happening.

Meanwhile, back in the kitchen, Mom and Dad were lost in their own thoughts. Each came to the conclusion that the time had come to share Grammy P.'s dementia diagnosis with Millie.

They agreed to tell Millie what it would mean for their family. This was something they had avoided talking about.
But it had become clear they couldn't avoid this conversation any longer. They needed to share the changes Millie was starting to see and could expect to see in the future.

Dad stayed behind to clean up the kitchen while Mom headed to the living room to help Grammy P. get ready for bed.

Millie returned to the kitchen to help Dad for a couple of minutes.

Mom reentered the kitchen. "Millie, it's time to go up and get ready for bed."

"Why can't Grammy P. remember how to play Trouble®?" Millie asked, both parents.

"Millie, let's wait until we get upstairs to talk," replied Mom.

Both parents wanted to have a private conversation with Millie, one Grammy P could not overhear.

Mom and Millie headed upstairs with Dad promising to join them soon.

When they got upstairs, Millie said, “That was so not fun.”

“I know honey. You love game time and I’m sorry it didn’t go as expected,” Mom said.

Mom explained that Grammy P.’s memory was causing her to forget the rules.

“But Grammy P. has always had a GREAT memory! That’s what you say anyway.”

“Let’s get ready for bed and Dad will come up soon and join us and we can read a bedtime story,” Mom suggested.

Millie!

Dad joined Mom and Millie in her bedroom, one on both sides of her bed. This was not unusual because the three chatted every night before sleep. First, they gave Millie a big hug.

Then they explained, "Grammy P. now has a sickness that causes her to forget things quickly. It's called dementia, which means gradual memory loss, loss of sense of smell and taste, lack of desire for activities, loss of ability to walk or move around, and loss of ability to take care of yourself. Grammy P. will need help eating, bathing, brushing her teeth, and going to the bathroom one day."

"Some dementia patients repeat their sentences because they don't remember they have said them before. And it could eventually mean that Grammy P. may forget who her family is. It's like no matter how many memories they put in, the memories kind of drain out the bottom."

Dad and Mom continued to explain that not only Grammy P.'s memory will go away but that she may be sad and angry when that happens.

"It has nothing to do with you or us sweetie", said Mom. She further stated, "I'm still trying to understand this whole thing myself."

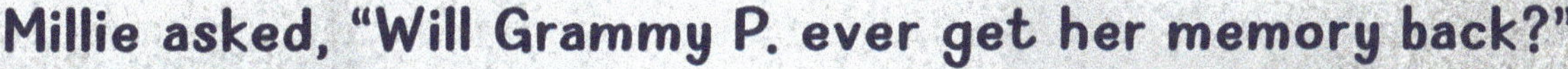

Millie asked, "Will Grammy P. ever get her memory back?"

Both parents glanced at one another and then back at Millie.

"Unfortunately, no Sweetie. We hope someday that the Alzheimer's Association will help to find a cure for dementia but they haven't found one yet.

"In the meantime, we need to love on Grammy P. extra hard as this is a very difficult disease.

"Dementia is sad for Grammy P., our entire family, and friends who also love Grammy P."

"But we had so much fun at the beach when I was little," persisted Millie hoping some memories would stay longer with Grammy P.

"That's the funny thing about dementia. Some memories do stay. We just don't know which ones will stay or for how long," said Dad.

"How did she get dementia anyway?" asked Millie

"We don't know Sweetie Pie but our job," said Dad, "Is kindness. We will show kindness to Grammy P. And respect. And always love."

"I can do that!" said Millie.

"Yes you can," agreed Mom. "We will help each other."

The next morning before school, Millie headed to visit Grammy P. in the living room to say goodbye just like she had done every day Grammy P. stayed over.
Mom was already there encouraging Grammy P. to get ready to start the day. Meanwhile, Dad headed to the living room with the coffee he had prepared for his usual morning exchanges with Grammy P.

Millie gave Grammy P. a big hug while smiling at Mom. "Good Morning!" she said to both Grammy P. and Mom.

When Grammy P. repeated herself, Millie looked at Mom over Grammy P.'s shoulder.
Mom smiled her encouragement to Millie.
Millie refrained from saying, "Grammy P., you just said that!"
They embraced and said goodbye
to start their days.

MILLIE'S BIGGER STORY

Millie's Grandmother -- Grammy P.-- was diagnosed with dementia when Millie was barely two years old. Millie was too young to notice the gradual changes in Grammy P. But that changed when Grammy P. could no longer hide her cognitive challenges.

That fateful night, when our family played a Trouble ® game with Grammy P., was a turning point for all of us. So, we wrote this story for you so you know that children from 2 and above can feel the impact of a loved one's dementia journey and find enhanced ways to love and communicate during memory loss.

Before Millie's eyes, her relationship with Grammy P. changed. She struggled to understand why her grandmother could no longer communicate and play with her as she used to.

Wise Millie also witnessed the struggles and emotional exchanges between her parents and Grammy P. as her parents learned how to embrace their new caregiver roles and deal with the losses dealt by dementia.

Grammy P. battled dementia for seven years. Her experiences included having multiple caregivers who supported her 24 hours a day. She could no longer visit Millie and her parents at their home. Dinner and board games with Grammy P. became a thing of the past. Instead, the family had to visit Grammy P. Special memories included hugs between Grammy P. and Millie, reading Bible verses, and sharing with Grammy P. how much Millie loved her.

In the end, Millie was devastated by losing Grammy P. and grappled with understanding why dementia had to be so cruel and steal Grammy P. away. The family continues to honor Grammy P's legacy by talking about and remembering her daily.

This book is a tribute to Grammy P., emphasizing the family connections formed that evening over a board game.

Answer the questions below to show your knowledge.

Dementia is a memory loss disease that affects millions globally.

True or False?

QUESTION

There is a cure for dementia

True or False?

Families, by themselves, can care for loved ones with dementia.

True or False? Why?

QUESTION

Talking about a loved one having dementia is a no/no. You must only talk with family members about dementia

True or False? Why?

There are many ways to show love despite dementia

True or False?
What are Some?

Find answers in the resource section at www.remembermegrammyP.com

WAYS FAMILIES CAN SUPPORT LOVED ONES DIAGNOSED WITH DEMENTIA

1-Spend time with loved ones. When visiting with children, make visits short and sweet. Don't force children to engage as they may become confused, resentful, or distant.

2-Give kids ideas on how to communicate with someone who has dementia. For example, show kids how they can use music as a connector to build happy memories.

Another example is sharing toys like a Pop It fidget toy that allows fingers to be involved as an activity.

3-Pay attention when you or family members are feeling angry. Take a time out if you need to. Sing a song if that helps. Do something fun separately as a family to re-connect and re-energize before re-engaging with someone suffering from dementia.

SIMONE'S STORY

My mom, a.k .a. Grammy P., was my rock for as long as I can remember. She was there for every special moment in my life. She's the one person I would call to share my highs and lows. I can't articulate enough how painful this dementia journey has been for me and my loved ones. I have had to lean heavily on my family's love during times when my mom's sickness overwhelms me, and I feel utterly helpless.

I became concerned when I noticed a change in her behavior and cognitive abilities. The night we played the board game was a turning point moment for our family. Before that, we never gave a diagnosis or name to dementia in conversations with Millie.

Grammy P. was not receptive to my help when I began bringing her to the memory doctor, citing my concerns. One day, she had an outburst in the doctor's office, sharing that I was trying to say she was "crazy" and put her in an asylum. Her words hurt me deeply, and at the time, I didn't understand it was dementia impacting her words and actions. So, I took it as a personal attack and withdrew, feeling disillusioned and disappointed.

As I said, I took a step back from the situation. But Mom (Grammy P.) continued to change over the years. Others in the family took note. I then re-engaged and got her officially diagnosed. It was one of the most challenging things I've had to do.

You see, I lacked the skills to care for my mom correctly, and I knew zilch about dementia. I found it challenging to balance all my family and entrepreneurial responsibilities and summon what was needed to be a caregiver. I felt overwhelmed navigating this space. Thankfully, I've found outlets to release my anger and frustration about dementia. I'm fortunate to have support for my mental well-being. And this book serves as a therapeutic outlet for my creativity.

In time, we had no choice but to adjust to a new normal with dementia ever-present. Support was necessary to deal with the pain, but Grammy P. needed our unconditional love for this journey. Losing Grammy P in February 2024 was deeply painful for our family. We continue to process the huge loss and find ways to educate others about dealing with dementia. We plan to participate in the annual Alzheimer's Walk and Run to honor Grammy P.'s legacy.

DEMENTIA RESOURCES

RESOURCE	WHAT?	HOW TO FIND IT?
Alzheimer's Association	An educational resource that serves as a one-stop shop to learn about dementia. In addition, there are many caregiving resources available from The Alzheimer's Association.	https://www.alz.org/help-support Information for Teens https://www.alz.org/help-support/resources/kids-teens/for_teens Information for Kids https://www.alz.org/help-support/resources/kids-teens/for_kids
Walk to End Alzheimer's	A national activity for families and friends to amplify the need for a cure for Alzheimer's and Dementia. This is a great way to raise funds to support finding a cure for Dementia.	www.walktoendalz.com
YouTube	YouTube sources educational online videos that provide dementia education and resources. Here are some helpful search phrases on the platform: "What is dementia," or "dementia: how children learn to understand."	www.youtube.com
Library	Find books and media on dementia and other memory challenges. Ask your librarians for help. They may know what helped other families. Or they may know key words or places to search that are not immediately apparent.	www.Google.com and input the word *library* to find your local library.
Therapy	Connect with therapists who specialize in handling Alzheimer's/Dementia. This can be a great resource for tips for adults who are guiding children. Additionally, engage with pediatricians for children's therapy conversations to better process dementia.	www.psychology.com Call your pediatrician's office or check the pediatrician's website. Check with www.alz.org, as they also have a resource for counselors for children.
***Remember Me, Grammy P.* Resource Site**	We've created a site to provide ongoing resources that help families supporting loved ones with dementia. Here, you can download our *Remember Me, Grammy P.* discussion guide to support rich conversations on dementia. Also, download the answer keys to *Remember Me, Grammy P.* book activities.	www.remembermegrammyp.com

REMEMBER ME, GRAMMY P.

WORD SEARCH

```
T E M E N W K R H V V G P Q K R E Q C Y
O U I I M F F B E X J K E C F P O N E Z
G M D N L Q A X S L Q X K W O T U E O D
G U P R O L U M X D H M W C X R S I I Z
U N C B A Y I D I D W L W A A G F G R E
H D I N N E R E L L J J V Q L V V H A L
M G R A M M Y P X O Y L X C Z M E F Z R
M G F I R Y J T S H V P S A H K U O H J
O I F H D C Y T D Y V E G A E I K R G Y
T R T L E I W M R I B Q L X I N D G R L
P S Z U M I J M J O W H P I M D A I A S
O O D S E I L R O C U U G L E N D V Z A
N D J D N P N K Q M V B E P R E N E O K
Q M H D T L F N A I X C L I S S H W F Q
J M U W I W N H J J K B I E K S K H R V
K Q N H A C B E U M M J R Z V V I J O E
P S L C U E H Y Y N C D S E U P K S S Y
X Q Q W P X Z C P B P S N T V P H U Y X
U O L Y F B Y F V G G R K E A M A V V Y
X R E S P E C T R H F I H F T Z V F Z M
```

Alzheimers	Dementia	Kindness	Love	Millie
Grammy P	Forgive	Trouble	Mom	
Respect	Family	Dinner	Dad	

REMEMBER ME, GRAMMY P.

TROUBLE

More Acknowledgments

To Our Wonderful Illustrator, Audeva,
You are beyond talented.
Thank you for bringing the book to life with your beautiful imagery.
We loved creating Remember Me, Grammy P. with you.
We adore and appreciate you.

Thanks to our editor, Karen.
Your challenges and edits made the book a better resource.

To my best friend, B.,
Thanks for your continuing support in everything I do.
I appreciated sharing the Remember Me, Grammy P.
book journey with you. We love you.

To Team Simone Morris Enterprises LLC,
Thank you for letting me bounce ideas off you
in our team meetings.
We appreciate your behind-the-scenes input.

www.ingramcontent.com/pod-product-compliance
Ingram Content Group UK Ltd.
Pitfield, Milton Keynes, MK11 3LW, UK
UKHW052224270726
14059UKWH00003B/104

9 798989 897223